LENTFULNESS

40 ALL-AGE ACTIVITIES FOR LENT

ELEANOR KING

KEVIN MAYHEW LTD

First published in 2020 by Kevin Mayhew Ltd,
Rattlesden,
Stowmarket,
Suffolk, IP14 3BW
www.kevinmayhew.com

ISBN (paperback) 978-1-8385-8094-0
ISBN (eBook) 978-1-8385-8095-7
Paperback product code 1501674
eBook product code 1501675

Created with Vellum

With many thanks to my lovely family who are always such good company — my husband Matt, and my children Naomi, Toby and Clement.

CONTENTS

Introduction

YOU DON'T NEED TO START AT THE BEGINNING . . .

This is not the sort of book that you need to start at the beginning and work your way through (I often don't find myself reading books that way anyway!) Although there are forty sections, these can be dipped into and used in any order, in whichever way works best for you. Miss a few, do several together, adapt the ideas, or just read through it and mull over some of the thoughts as you go.

The idea is that the book is accessible for a range of different ages. As well as some thoughts, reflections, actions or activities to start you off at the beginning, there is something to pray, something to wonder about, and something to share for each section. These could be used as a family group at home, or would also work well as part of an online chat or video call.

I hope that this will enable you to find a little bit of space to reflect together in your journey through Lent, and provide a chance to wonder, rest, find peace, and receive God's blessing at this special time of year.

1

PANCAKE DAY

Pancake Day is one of the religious festivals that for some reason seems to have stood the test of time. If anything, like so many things for which purchasing is an important part, it has become more prominent, with supermarkets reminding us of the important date, friends sharing special toppings on social media, and children excited about how many pancakes they might be able to eat in one go.

Giving things up for Lent, too, is something that many people are still aware of. We can use our pancakes to wrap up the leftover chocolate spread so that we are not tempted by it later on, and to take the opportunity to enjoy the unhealthy treats that we know we really need to take a break from.

There is a growing awareness that perhaps there might be things we can do over Lent which can have a wider positive effect than making us a little slimmer for a few weeks, before all the Easter chocolate. Many people are giving up or reducing plastic use, or taking steps to live more sustainably and ethically.

Lent is also a time where some people collect an item a day for a food bank, or sort through the items of clothing that they do not need, and take them to a charity shop.

Alternatively, Lent might be the time to give to charity, perhaps collecting coins in a jar or fundraising for a particular project. Whatever we prayerfully decide to do, it is good to mark this special time of year as we prepare ourselves for Easter.

Something to pray

Lord,
as we cook our pancakes,
round and bubbling,
hot and sweet,
we pray that you would help us
show your love
to those we meet.

Amen

Something to wonder about

What is the most unusual filling for a pancake that you can imagine?

Something to share

What are your favourite pancake toppings?

2

ASH WEDNESDAY

The shops and supermarkets don't have any motivation to promote Ash Wednesday, however, as nobody needs to buy anything for it! Traditionally, churches burn the palm crosses from last year and mix this ash with oil, using this to mark the sign of a cross on people's foreheads.

As, of course, Ash Wednesday falls in the middle of the working week, and not all churches do an evening service, it can be something that people can miss out on when they are at the busiest stage of their lives. In response to this, some churches have been going outside with their pot of ash, offering ash crosses to people going about their daily lives. This short yet powerful interaction can be a real blessing for people wanting to connect with the spiritual side of their lives, and can be a wonderful opportunity for prayer and conversation, as well as making the church activities more visible.

On Ash Wednesday, it is a time to think about the things in our lives with which we need some help from God. Coming before God in honesty and humility can be an opportunity for healing, peace and refreshment. Some people like to talk and pray with someone, or make their confession at this time. But whether we do this or not, we could all do with spending time with God, openly bringing these things in our lives before him, knowing that we need his wisdom and strength.

Something to pray

Dear Lord,
with dusty ash
we make a cross,
a sign upon our head.
We leave behind
our selfishness
and choose kindness
instead.

Amen.

Something to wonder about

How would you feel about having an ash cross on your head? Would you walk around outside with it on, or wash it off?

Something to share

If you could choose a gift from God to help you in your life, would you most like to receive wisdom, patience, understanding, generosity, love, or something else?

3

MINIMALISM

Minimalism has become very popular. Many people see the images of a beautiful, clear, tidy home and feel that this is something that will bring them peace. This tells us something about our current society and culture. All this stuff around us, so easily available, and sold to us as if it will make our lives complete, is in fact doing the opposite.

This over-consumption is crippling the environment and is increasing inequality too. As people fill up their houses with more things, they often feel emptier. But how does this fit in with the Christian message? If we are clearing out our things and they are just going to landfill, and then we feel we can buy another, more expensive thing in its place, this is not helpful to us, or to anyone else. On the other hand, if we are able to find a good home for these items, where they can be appreciated and used again, this can help others.

We need to be careful that we are not just decluttering in order to be able to upgrade what we have. True simplicity sometimes does involve a little clutter, as we collect items for charity or recycling, grow our own vegetables in plastic pots we have saved, or mend and fix our old clothes.

Something to pray

Dear God,
we offer before you
all of our stuff.
In many ways
there's more than enough.

We pray
that you'll show us
your generous way
so our things are a blessing,
not just thrown away.

Amen.

Something to wonder about

If you had a box to fill, and this was all you could keep, what would you put in it?

Something to share

Everyone can choose an item, preferably something which is worn out, empty or ready to be thrown away. How could this item have another life, and continue to be useful? Perhaps paper or empty containers could be made into pots to plant seeds.

Could a plastic box become an instrument, when elastic bands are stretched around it? And old clothes could have the buttons saved, and be cut into pieces to be dusters or to make something new. If the items are too far gone for this, find out about how they can be made into new things at the recycling plant

4

HUMAN INTERACTION

It's great to be able to find out how to get somewhere by looking up maps on the internet, to translate things, work out what's on, and read the news. We have so much access to information and the ability to find out the answers to anything we like. But however useful this may be, perhaps sometimes it is good to take the chance to wonder about things, to talk with others about what they think, and to mull it over. When we choose to ask others rather than look up the answer straight away, we get so many other benefits.

Through that human interaction, and the other person knowing that it is something we are interested in, this may lead to other links and interesting conversations.

We may also find that we uncover more layers to our answer that we thought were there at first. Are there things we might usually look up on the internet which we could instead have an interesting conversation about with someone we have not spoken to for a while, or someone who may live alone and would appreciate that human conversation and contact?

Something to pray

Loving God,
thank you for our community
and our family,
far and near.

And thank you
for friends
and neighbours
as we learn together
and share.

Amen.

Something to wonder about

Wonder together about some interesting questions such as:

- 'Will we be able to talk to animals one day? And what would they say?'
- 'If you invented a creature to live in the desert, what would it be like?'
- 'Does the Universe have an edge, and if it does, what would be the other side of it?'

Something to share

Talk about who you would ask to find out about the best chocolate brownie recipe, how to say something in another language, what to pack for going camping, or to find out what life was really like in Roman times.

5

BORED?

'I'm not bored now!' my 11 year old announced today. 'Because here there are lots of things to do!' We weren't at an amusement park, cinema, or exciting swimming pool. There were not any shiny magazines, computer games or sports equipment. We'd stopped where there was a square of grass to play on, with a path around the edge, and he was making up running and chasing games to play with his cousins.

Perhaps we underestimate our children and young people's capacity to appreciate the simple things in life, thinking that they will need ever more elaborate ways to be entertained and kept from boredom. We have a lot to learn from the baby scrunching a bit of bright fabric, the toddler banging a saucepan, the children playing 'it' or hide and seek, and the teenagers enjoying the swings and roundabouts at the park.

What are the ordinary things and simple things around us which we can really appreciate today?

Something to pray

Thank you, Lord,
for space to 'be'.
For the wide blue sky
and the shade of a tree.

Thank you
for when we can share
cake and tea
and for time with our friends
and family.

Amen.

Something to wonder about

Do you think people were more or less bored in Stone Age Times than they are now? What might they have done back then to keep the boredom at bay – and would they have needed to?

Something to share

What are your favourite places, and favourite things to do? What is it that makes these things special?

6

GOD'S LOVE

At the moment I have a temporary tattoo of the delicate and beautiful chemical structure of the amazing hormone, oxytocin, on my arm.

Oxytocin helps a new mum and baby to bond with each other as they spend time close together. It gives that wonderful feeling of love and happiness, and is released particularly strongly when a mother holds her baby next to her own skin after birth.

Understanding the scientific explanation of something does not disprove or invalidate the human experience of it, but can actually help us to appreciate it more. The Bible talks about us knowing and experiencing God's love and care for us like a baby on its mother's breast.

As we draw near to God in prayer, let's not rush away, but spend time enjoying that closeness in his love.

Something to pray

Holy Spirit,
our comfort,
we rest in your love,
receiving your healing
and peace from above.

Amen

Something to wonder about

What does it feel like to experience God's comforting love? Is it something you could describe or explain to others?

Something to share

What are the things which bring a feeling of comfort and care, and show us something of God's love?

Perhaps hugging a teddy, sharing a book together on the sofa with someone, being handed a hot drink or given a home-made cake, or wrapping a blanket around your shoulders. How can we help share these things with others too?

7

FOOD BANKS

Some people are collecting 40 items in 40 days to donate to a local food bank or homeless shelter. This can be quite a satisfying and practical thing to do over the season of Lent. It can also lead us to think about the many complex reasons behind the huge rise in food bank use, and wonder what we might do if we were in those challenging circumstances. We may be tempted to start to think about how we would try to avoid those problems in the first place. However, we know there are such complex and multi-layered issues leading people to end up in difficult situations, and it is never simply down to any individual event.

When we think about the way in which Jesus met and spoke with others, whatever their history, background or circumstances, he saw them as a valued human being and as a loved and precious child of God.

As we collect our items to donate, let's thank God for the people who will receive them, and pray that they would know his blessing.

Something to pray

Generous God,
help us to be generous, too.
With gifts,
time,
and kind words,
may your love
shine through.

Amen.

Something to wonder about

Why is there inequality? There is both wealth and poverty at a community level, nationally and internationally. Does this have a negative effect just on those who are poor, or is it also bad for those who are rich as well?

Something to share

What would you most like to donate to a food bank and why?

8

CLEARING OUT

Another Lent discipline is to look around your house and find 40 things, or bags of things, that you do not need, and to give these away to a charity shop so that they can be enjoyed by someone else.

The great thing about charity shops is that everyone wins – the person who is clearing out their house gains space, the charity shop raises money for a good cause, the person buying the item finds something that they need at a good price, it prevents rubbish going to landfill, and reduces the amount of things that people need to buy brand new. However, as we find something to take to the charity shop, we need to be careful that we are not just clearing out so that we can go shopping for new items and fill our house up again.

The fashion industry has a huge environmental impact. First let's consider if we really need the new item. If so, we may be able to buy something second-hand, borrow something or adapt an item which we already have. After this, we might consider buying from a retailer which has high environmental and ethical standards. As this is not always possible, we will probably end up buying a few essential items from the mainstream shops, but this will be a lot less than it might have been.

Something to pray

Lord Jesus,
when we think of what you had
when you lived on earth
it was not that much.
Simple clothes, tools, food,
and a home which was probably not that big.

Your furniture might have been quite nice:
simple but handmade and good quality
coming from a family of carpenters.
If things broke you probably fixed them
yourself
(or maybe asked your mum if it was a sewing
job).

Help us to remember this
when we look around our own home.
If we have extra, we can share with others
and if things are broken, perhaps we can fix
them too.

Amen.

Something to wonder about

Thinking about the items you are going to donate, imagine who might be enjoying them or using them after you. What age might the person be, and what are they like?

After that, think about what might happen to the things next – perhaps they would be given back to the charity shop and someone else would be able to use them, or they might be made into something else.

Something to share

What is your favourite second-hand item that you have and why?

9

SAYING THANK YOU

Lent can be a good time to show our appreciation to the people who do very important jobs in our community. There is a good awareness of the important role that nurses, firefighters and paramedics have, and this is rightly acknowledged.

There are, however, plenty of other people who also work really hard in essential jobs, but who are often ignored, and are sometimes subject to verbal abuse.

Perhaps we could use Lent as an opportunity to get into the habit of thanking the people who collect our rubbish and sweep our streets, those who work as delivery drivers, cleaners, people who maintain our roads, and security staff.

If we want to learn from Jesus' example, he paid no attention to people's worldly status or wealth, but valued each person just for who they were.

Something to pray

Dear God,
we're so thankful
for the people who help us.

For those who look after our water
and energy supply,
who clean our streets,
schools,
healthcare settings
and transport.

We're grateful for those who work
to provide our food,
and those who bring it to us.

For those who look after others,
young and old,
and for all others who look after us.
May they be blessed in all they do.

Amen.

Something to wonder about

What would it be like if the rubbish collectors stopped work this week?

What about the delivery drivers or the cleaners, or the people who look after our electricity or water supply?

Something to share

What essential jobs have you seen being done in your community this week?

10

FASTING

Lent has traditionally been a time of fasting – an important discipline in many religions. It is interesting to see that fasting has recently become more popular as a part of various diets, but this is with an emphasis on self-improvement and losing weight rather than as a tool to draw near to God.

If you already fast as part of a diet, use it as an opportunity to pray. As you make the choice to go without something that you would really like to eat, take a step into God's presence and receive spiritual nourishment from him. If you don't already fast, try eating a meal thoughtfully, prayerfully and thankfully, as a chance to focus on God.

Something to pray

Lord God,
when we eat and drink
may we do it thoughtfully

and thankfully,
not greedily,
hurriedly
or taking it for granted.

And whether we eat a big meal,
or whether we eat a small one,
may we do it in your company.

Amen.

Something to wonder about

If you had to have the same meal for dinner forever, what would it be?

Something to share

What food would you find it hardest to go without? Cheese or carrots? Chocolate or chips? Pizza or pasta? Yoghurt or ice cream? What about bread or potatoes?

11

FOOD

In the past, meat free meals were an important part of Lent, and this can be an easy and practical way to mark the season as well as to get into the habit of eating and shopping in a way which is gentler on the environment.

Think about ways of using seasonal and local vegetables, and plant protein such as beans, lentils and peas, along with some brown rice, pasta or baked potatoes.

If we all make a shift in our eating habits so that if we do eat meat, it is only a couple of times a week, this would have a massive positive impact on our world, and there would be enough food for everyone both now and in the future.

Something to pray

Lord,
we thank you
for hot and tasty beans,
sweet and crunchy carrots

bright, juicy tomatoes,
fragrant, filling rice,
and fluffy baked potatoes.

We are so grateful
for the delicious food
which grows
on your good earth.

Amen.

Something to wonder about

Find out the environmental impact of (for example) a meat burger compared to a vegetarian burger. Why do you think this is?

Something to share

Play a game, starting with the words 'In my delicious steaming soup, I put ...' Each person can add an ingredient in turn, and you need to try to remember and repeat the list of the ingredients that were said before your turn!

12

SPEAKING AND LISTENING

Social media can be great – a way to connect with others who we would not otherwise see very often, and a way to find out things that are going on. It can be tempting, though, to get into the habit of engaging with it on and off throughout the day. Sometimes those few words posted by someone can seem to hold much more weight and importance than if they were spoken in passing, in a conversation.

We need to make sure that we are valuing the conversations and interactions that we have in real life as least as much as the conversations that are happening on social media.

Let's take the opportunity to listen – really listen – to those people we come across today.

Something to pray

Lord Jesus,
thank you for the way

we can talk to you.

Help us to listen as you do,
showing people
that their stories are worth hearing,
showing that we care
and that you love them too.

Amen.

Something to wonder about

What chances do we have to speak to people in person during the day – whether for a chat or simply to say hello?

Something to share

Have we ever met a person by coincidence, and ended up having an interesting or useful conversation with them?

13

LOVED AS WE ARE

However much we try not to, there is always the temptation to compare ourselves to others on social media.

This might be in terms of appearance, achievement, success or popularity. We may find ourselves starting to feel that we are not good enough in comparison to others.

This feeling is not from God. It is something that can lead us to making bad choices. God loves us so much and we are precious to him.

As we spend time in his loving company we can start to realise that his love for us is not dependent on what we look like, how busy, successful or glamorous we are, or how many friends we have.

Let's turn off the screen for a little while and receive that love.

Something to pray

Lord Jesus,
when we are with you
we know that we don't have to pretend
and it's not a competition.

You don't love us any more,
or any less,
because of the state of our hair,
our skin,
our clothes,
or our general appearance.

You love us completely,
already,
and all we have to do
is to be ourselves:

ordinary but unique,
wonderful and complex,
loved and lovable,
known by you.

Amen.

Something to wonder about

If Jesus was walking around our community today, what would we like to show him, and what would we tell him? Who would he spend time to stop and talk with?

Something to share

Using the letters in each person's name, create an acrostic poem of their characteristics. For example:

Courageous
Loving
Excellent
Making
Exploring
Nature-loving
Thoughtful

14

ISOLATION

We may have friends or family who rely on social media for contact, and to be part of a community, because of isolation caused by illness or disability. This can be a really important thing which helps people to cope with tough circumstances.

We can remember these people and think of things that would interest them and encourage them, perhaps posting pictures of these and tagging them in. Of course, personal messages are always appreciated too, and it may be that we could send some pictures or a friendly email or message as well.

Something to pray

Lord,
we pray for those we care about
living all alone.

May our messages bring comfort,
sent by letter or by phone.

May your loving arms
surround them
so they know
that they are hugged
and as part of your big family
know that they
are loved.

Amen.

Something to wonder about

Who do you know who is isolated and would appreciate a picture or a message?

Something to share

Think about what these people might like and take a photo, draw a picture or write a message for them.

15

PERSONAL MESSAGES

Perhaps Lent could be a time to send 40 personal messages to people? This might be more than one to the same person if it works out that way. Social media has changed the way in which we tell our news to our friends, and instead of it being a personal interaction, considering the circumstances and experiences of the individual listener, we now tend to broadcast one version of our lives to both our close friends and our passing acquaintances.

Sending individual messages, texts, letters, emails or postcards can be a way to show that we value our relationship with that person, and the experiences which we have shared together.

Something to pray

Lord God,
you created us,
and you know us all.

Some of us big,
and some of us small.

Unique
and individual.

Amen.

Something to wonder about

How did people keep in touch before social media was around? How often did the post arrive, and were there different things which arrived through the letterbox?

What about using the telephone – how is that different now to how it was in the past? What does this mean for our communication with others?

Something to share

If you could choose only one way to keep in touch with people who live far away, what would it be – writing letters, phone calls, email, social media, text messages, or something else?

16

THE ENVIRONMENT

Campaigning on environmental and social issues is something that has been made very convenient through the technology which has now become part of normal life. Lent could be a time to sign up for campaign updates so that we can be involved in pushing for change that will help to make the world a better place.

Craftivism has the same objective, but in a very different way. Through careful, slow-paced, creative activity, craftivists make their point in a way which is radically different, gentle yet powerful, and difficult to ignore.

Something to pray

Creator God,
we thank you
for our world
so bright and round.

For the plants and trees
you've blessed us with
which grow in the good ground.

For the sparkling salty water
stretching far across the sea,
a home for many creatures
and beautiful to see.

We're grateful for the clear, crisp air
and clouds in the sky above,
and we pray that you would help us care,
strengthened by your love.

Amen.

Something to wonder about

Sometimes all the issues in the world can seem overwhelming, and we don't know where to start to make a difference. What might you be actually able to do in your real life circumstances? Have a think about what this might be, and choose a small action to complete today.

Something to share

Spend a bit of time creating a picture, embroidery, poster or other artwork together to raise awareness of an important issue

17

CREATION

All around us there are things which are interesting and beautiful, even if it doesn't always feel that way. God has given us so many good things to bless us and make our world beautiful.

Take a phone or camera, and find ten beautiful things within ten minutes' walk of where you live, and thank God for these.

Whether you find a determined dandelion, an interesting tree trunk, a bright, textured sky or an old brick wall covered in moss and ivy, recognising and valuing these things can bring us close to God in thankfulness and praise.

Something to pray

Wonderful God,
maker of the universe,
your fingerprints are shown
in all creation!

The stretching branches of the trees.
The wide, ever-changing sky.
The tiny flower petals
and the veins in leaves,
different, yet from the same pattern.

All these things are so beautiful,
and we thank you.

Amen.

Something to wonder about

Why are some beautiful things in nature given higher value and status than other things? What would be your 'big 5' of plants or creatures to spot in your community?

Something to share

What surprised you during the photo walk activity, and did you notice anything you hadn't seen before?

18

TODAY'S PROPHETS

The Old Testament prophets bravely spoke out about things which were not right, and needed to be changed. Confident in their relationship with God, they were able to have those difficult conversations and make a stand on important issues whether this was well received, or whether it made them unpopular. They also often used actions as well as words to get their points across.

Who are the prophets in our world today, speaking out truth to power? These might be people inside or outside the church.

Are there issues on which we know we need to use our voice to speak out, rather than keeping quiet for an easy life? This might be in something quite small, perhaps through supporting an important cause in their campaign. But together we can make a difference.

Something to pray

Lord God,
help us use our voices
to speak out for what is right,
to stand up for those who are not heard,
and to make a difference.

Amen.

Something to wonder about

Which people or organisations are speaking out for equality, peace and justice? Is this happening within the church, outside the church, or both?

Something to share

Together, make a donation or take an action to support an organisation campaigning on an important issue such as environmental, social or health justice.

19

LIFE'S DIRECTION

Labyrinths and mazes have been around a long time. They are also associated with helping us think about our spiritual journey through life, too.

Visit a maze, and as you walk around it, take time to think about the way that life sometimes takes us in different directions, but with the same goal at the end. As you find the end of the maze, thank God for the way that he is always beside us wherever we go.

Something to pray

Thank you, dear Lord,
for the way you walk beside us.

The way you lead us
and the way you encourage us
in our journey through life.

It is so good to know
that we can travel in your company
and whatever life throws at us
we are never alone.

Amen.

Something to wonder about

Is life more like a maze (which has different routes and dead ends) or a labyrinth (which twists and turns, and goes back on itself, but takes you to the finish along its winding path)

Something to share

Each person can look up an online picture of a maze or labyrinth and share it with everyone else

20

LISTENING TO OTHERS

Lent can be a time for us to practise listening – really listening – to others. Sometimes, when people are telling us about their lives, it is easy to be tempted to interrupt with some story of a similar thing which has happened to us.

Perhaps we could try holding that experience in our mind, but using it as a way to empathise with and understand the other person more, giving them the chance to tell us about their own experiences.

To be a good friend like this is a wonderful gift to give, and can make all the difference to someone who is facing challenges in their life.

Something to pray

Loving God,
spending time in your company,
we know that you care,

we can talk about good things,
and what's been unfair.

May the way that you listen
teach us to do
this in the same way
that we've now learnt from you.

Amen.

Something to wonder about

Do you like talking, listening or both? Does it depend on who you are with?

Something to share

Try taking it in turns for one person to talk for two minutes, and everyone else to listen. What was this like?

21

LISTENING TO GOD

We can also use Lent as a time to practise listening to God. Sometimes our prayer can involve a lot of talking, perhaps of asking God for things. There is nothing wrong with this, and it is lovely to be able to tell God about all the things we are happy about, the things that are troubling us, and all that we are thinking and feeling.

Perhaps through Lent, we could take a few minutes every day just to be with God? Not talking, not asking, not saying any words but just resting in his stillness and love. We may be surprised that this is easier than we thought, and find that we experience closeness with God in a different way than we have done before.

Something to pray

Holy God,
in the stillness of your presence,

we find peace,
we find love,
we find comfort,
and we find hope.

Thank you for the precious time
we can spend in your company.

Amen.

Something to wonder about

Set a timer for one minute, and sit together in silence (if you can!). Does the time seem to go more quickly or more slowly? Why do you think this is? Did you notice any sounds in the background?

Something to share

Would you rather live in a noisy place or a quiet place? Why? And would it depend on what sort of noise it was?

22

SIGNS

When you walk around outside, look to see if there are any things in the environment around you which speak to you about the Easter story. Perhaps there are some tree roots breaking through concrete, reminding us of God's resurrection power. Perhaps there are cross shapes hidden in the brickwork, among the joins between paving stones in the floor, in wrought iron fences or in the wispy trails of aeroplanes crossing paths in the sky.

There may also be stones which remind you of the one which covered the tomb where Jesus was buried, or little clumps of colourful spring flowers and green grass which remind you of the garden where Jesus first appeared to his friends.

Take note of these and thank God for them. You might also like to take photos of these as an aid to prayer during Lent and Holy Week.

Something to pray

Lord Jesus,
we thank you for the signs of new life
springing all around.

The trees all dressed in blossom.
The green shoots on the ground.

We pray
that as we hear
the Easter story,
we'd grow too,
being strengthened and refreshed,
from drawing near to you.

Amen.

Something to wonder about

In non-religious Easter springtime celebrations (eggs, flowers, new green leaves, bunnies, chicks etc.), are there things can we learn about God?

Something to share

What colours do you think about when you think of Spring? Choose three each, finding pictures or objects to show to each other.

23

EASTER CARDS

As we near Easter, it might be a good time to think about sending an Easter card with a letter inside to a friend or relative whom we have not spoken to for a while. These special occasions remind us to contact people who we do not often see, and as Easter is generally a quieter and less busy time than Christmas, it can be a good opportunity to take a little longer over writing a personal letter to someone.

Often older friends and relatives can miss out on news if they are not connected on social media, but as well as this, a letter written specially for someone shows care and interest in a way that a social media post written for a wider audience cannot do.

Something to pray

Dear God,
we pray with all our heart
for those from whom we are apart.

We pray they'd know
they're loved by you,
hugged by your arms,
just like we'd do.

Amen.

Something to wonder about

How did people keep in touch thirty years ago, one hundred years ago, or one thousand years ago? How would people have felt when they did hear news from a friend or relative?

Something to share

Who would you most like to get a letter from (this could be someone real, past or present, or someone fictional)

24

SPRING CLEAN

For those of us in the northern hemisphere, Lent falls within the season of Spring, a time traditionally associated with 'Spring Cleaning' (presumably because the newly appearing rays of sunshine suddenly shed light on and reveal the dusty patches which were there all along!) Wherever we live, a little spring cleaning can be good for us spiritually too. It might seem daunting to attempt to tackle the whole house. But sorting out one drawer or cupboard, or organising some files on the computer might be doable.

As we do this, we can think about where we would like God to help us spring clean in our hearts, too. Are there any cobwebs of bad habits or dust balls of judgemental thoughts? Perhaps we can ask God to help us with these today.

Something to pray

Dear Lord,
we bring our lives to you

the neat bits
and the messy bits too.

Please help us
as we sort things through
and live the way
you want us to.

Amen.

Something to wonder about

How does it feel to tell God about the untidy or messy bits in our lives? Is this easy or hard?

Something to share

Would you rather keep everything forever, or have to always get rid of things the same day?

25

LIFE'S DIFFICULTIES

Make a cross out of a couple of sticks or twigs. These don't need to be big at all. Tie them together with a piece of wire, wool or string. As you hold this cross, remember that Jesus understands our suffering. He knows what it is like to be in physical pain and to be exhausted. He also experienced having friends betray him and having the crowds turn against him. The soldiers, too, made fun of him. Suffering and pain is, sadly, sometimes part of life.

It is not something that God makes us go through, or something that he unkindly 'allows', but just is a natural consequence of living in a world where humans have free will.

Not everyone will make kind or sensible choices, and we cannot force others to act in a particular way, even if we would really like them to. What we can change, though, is ourselves. As we look towards God for strength, he will give us the wisdom, courage and comfort to get through whatever life throws at us.

Something to pray

Lord Jesus,
when things are difficult
we come to you in prayer.

You hold us close,
and listen,
with your reassuring care.

Thank you so much for loving us
and thanks for being there.

Amen.

Something to wonder about

Some people of faith have been through really tough times in their lives, but trust God more than ever. Other people look at this and wonder how God can allow suffering, feeling that this would be a reason to reject faith. What would you say to this?

Something to share

What are the things which bring comfort when life is difficult or sad?

26

THANKING GOD

Throughout Jesus' time of fasting in the desert, he never lost sight of his Father in Heaven. Through the most difficult times in our lives, we too can be sustained by this relationship.

God loves us and is always ready to listen to us. We can tell him all the things that concern us. But what can really can give us strength through the toughest times is to take the time to praise and thank God.

As counter-intuitive as this may seem, it is the one action which can make a massive transforming difference when nothing else will. Start by thanking God for what you can see around you – out loud if this helps.

These can be the simplest things. Thank him for his promises, and thank him for his blessings. Thank him for ordinary things like having running water and for the leaves on the trees. And see what happens.

Something to pray

Loving God,
we thank you
for the good things we can see.

For clean water,
for food and clothes,
and a land where there is peace.

For those in our community,
our friends and family,
who bless us with their presence
and their generosity.

Amen.

Something to wonder about

Being thankful or appreciative is helpful by itself – but is there something unique and different about having someone to be thankful to?

Something to share

Take turns to share something you are thankful for (this could be anything at all, big or small), starting with the words 'Thank you God, for ...' Continue taking it in turns, repeating the previous people's contributions, as well as your own, for as long as you can!

27

THE CROSS

Find a couple of small sticks or pieces of wood, and bind these together with string into a cross shape. Take some sandpaper, and as you smooth away the splinters and prickles, think about how God does this for us.

It is not always easy and we do not always want to let go of our unkind thoughts and selfish habits, but if we offer them to God we will feel better for it.

When you have finished sanding the wood so that it is smooth, you can use your cross as a 'holding cross' to help in prayer.

Something to pray

Lord God,
it's so easy
to pretend that everything is fine.

To justify our choices

so that we feel we are in the right.

Today we bring all our thoughts, opinions,
words and actions before you.

Because now
we're ready to listen,
we're ready to learn,
we choose to live
with love.

Amen.

Something to wonder about

What are the things which can make wood smooth? Are there things like this in our lives, too, which can smooth off our rough edges?

Something to share

Share your favourite textures – are there fabrics people do or don't like? What about different natural surfaces – sand, stone or wood?

28

PRAYER BRACELET

Make a prayer bracelet out of some stretchy jewellery thread and some wooden beads. When you have made it the right size for your wrist, tie a knot in the thread. Onto this, add an extra bead. This is so that you can feel the beginning and the end of the bracelet, without looking.

You might like to simply say the name of Jesus as you hold each bead in turn, starting and finishing at the marker bead. As you work your way around the circle and come back to the beginning, there will be a sense of completion.

This can be a simple way of finding a few minutes to spend in prayer during the day, and a way of drawing close to God and finding strength from him.

Something to pray

Jesus,
just by saying your name
we sense you are near.

Bringing joy to our hearts
and peace in our lives
as we spend time
with you.

Amen.

Something to wonder about

What other words might be helpful to say when using the beads for prayer or meditation?

Drawing on our knowledge of and relationship with Jesus, what words would you suggest to someone who wanted to try doing this, but was not happy with religious language?

Something to share

What names for Jesus can you think of, that are in the Bible?

29

EASTER FIRE

Some churches traditionally have a bonfire to welcome in Easter Day, either late on Easter Eve or early on Easter morning. Perhaps an Easter Eve bonfire might be a nice tradition to start – you could cook bananas wrapped in foil, with the first chocolate of Easter tucked away inside a slit in the banana!

Those bright and raw flames of fire in the darkness of that Easter Eve night bring us back to the message of God's power and victory over death.

With the scent of woodsmoke and the heat of the flames on your face, this ancient experience is a real contrast to the bunnies, pastel coloured eggs and fluffy chicks advertised and sold by the supermarkets – not that there's anything wrong with the bunnies and chicks of course, but hot, bright, unpredictable, lively fire is a deep and powerful symbol which can be helpful to us as we think about Easter, too.

Something to pray

Dear Lord,
the spark of new flame,
spreading across paper
and twigs
reminds us
of your victory
over death
and darkness.

The bright, dancing flames
of the fire
remind us of your Holy Spirit,
bringing life,
inspiration
and challenge
wherever we need it most.

And the glowing warmth
of the embers
tells us of your healing,
encouraging,
love.

Amen.

Something to wonder about

As you watch the fire, add fuel to it and tend to it, think about our ancestors through the ages who spent a lot of time doing this – their fire a source of warmth and light, a place to cook, somewhere to gather, something to look at and security. Which things in our modern life meet these needs today?

Something to share

How many different kinds of fire can you think of? Volcanoes, lightning, bonfires, incense, birthday candles, fireworks – what else can you add?

30

LIGHT A CANDLE

Create a Lenten focus for prayer using a candle, as well as a small jam jar filled with flowers, surrounded by some stones, shells or feathers. Light the candle, and set an alarm or phone timer for five minutes.

This time is yours, to rest and spend time in God's loving company. Breathe, and enjoy it. You don't need lots of words, and it doesn't matter if your mind wanders. It can be amazing how spacious that five minutes can be.

Something to pray

Lord,
as we light our candle
and spend some time with you
we're so glad that you love us
and we love you so much, too.

Amen.

Something to wonder about

What does it mean to have faith? To believe a certain set of things? To understand the world and life in a particular way? Is it about relationship and communication with God? A combination of these things, or something different altogether?

Something to share

What are your favourite small beautiful things in nature, and what are your favourite big beautiful things?

31

TAKING IT ALL IN

Get up early, if you can, and spend a little time outside. Look at the sky, and notice the different colours and shapes that you can see; if you were painting that sky, how many colours would you need? Feel the temperature of the air. See how the sky changes, even over the space of ten minutes or so – it might help to take a before and after photo. Listen out for the sounds of birds singing and people starting to get up and go about their business, and remember that we belong to this ongoing story, part way along the billions of mornings that the world has seen.

Something to pray

God of eternity,
creator of everything that there is,
and ever has been,
thank you for the beauty we see
and all that we experience

as we journey through our lives.
We are glad to have you as our friend!
It is so good to know
that we are loved
by you.

Amen.

Something to wonder about

Think about the spot where you are at this moment. What might it have been like one hundred years ago? What about a thousand years ago? Or ten thousand years ago?

Something to share

If there are clouds in the sky, see if you can spot any shapes in them, and share these with each other.

32

CHOCOLATE

As Easter approaches, the shops are full of chocolate eggs and sugary treats. Sometimes, if we leave it until nearly Easter to buy these things, most of them have already gone! Unless you have given up chocolate for Lent, and really don't want to break this, try taking one piece of really good, fairtrade chocolate, and eating it slowly and mindfully. Think about the beans that grew on the cocoa tree, and the farmers who harvested it. Don't try to do other things while you're eating the chocolate. Just concentrate on experiencing the texture, the flavour and the smell. Try not to think about eating the next piece while the first one is in your mouth, but enjoy the moment while you have it.

Something to pray

Creamy,
sweet
and fragrant

the chocolate
that we taste
reminds us of your goodness, Lord,
and your amazing grace.

Amen.

Something to wonder about

If chocolate didn't exist, what might take its place?

Something to share

If you could invent a new chocolate bar, what would it have in it?

33

TRADITIONS

Find out about Easter traditions around the world – there are many examples of special food being cooked and eaten, traditional gifts and customs, and plenty of symbolism. If you have particular cultures represented in your local community, find out what the Easter traditions are for these groups (if possible by asking people personally, a chance to learn and share and have interesting conversations).

Something to pray

Dear Lord,
there is so much that we can learn
and celebrate and share
as your family at Easter time
here and everywhere.

Amen.

Something to wonder about

What is your favourite Easter tradition? And if you made up a new tradition, what would it be?

Something to share

Everyone can look up a photo of an Easter food from around the world, and tell others about it. You might like to vote on your favourite!

34

PALM SUNDAY

Visit a donkey, if you can, or link up online with a donkey sanctuary and find out about what they do. Donkeys are still often treated badly throughout the world, and are taken for granted, expected to carry heavy loads over long distances without a rest. Jesus chose this humble creature to carry him on his journey into Jerusalem, as the people celebrated and praised him as a King. If you are able to stroke or pat a real-life donkey, remember what happened on Palm Sunday as you do this, and how Jesus chose an creature which was considered very ordinary to be part of a journey which went down in history.

Something to pray

Lord Jesus,
as you rode a gentle, humble donkey
you showed all of us
that you weren't the sort of king

who showed off about your wealth
your clothes
or how important you were.

And so we know
that there's no need for us
to show off about these things either.
Thank you that we can meet you
just as we are.

Amen.

Something to wonder about

What would it have been like to be part of the crowd on Palm Sunday? What might you have felt? And what could you see from where you were standing?

Something to share

Can you think of any other famous donkeys, either in the Bible or in other stories?

35

BREAD

Make some bread, perhaps with an ancient flour such as spelt, which was often used in Roman times. Form it into a circle, and mark a cross shape into the top with a knife.

When the bread is baked, share it with others, perhaps with other foods which would have been available in Roman times (olives, apples, dates, fish, sausages, cherries, peaches or plums). As you do this, imagine what it would have been like to share food together with Jesus.

Something to pray

Thank you, Lord,
for the bread we share
mixed together
and kneaded
with care.

Shaped with a cross,
baked till it smells good,
we're nourished and filled
by this wonderful food.

Amen.

Something to wonder about

What sort of things would Jesus have eaten? He often ate with others, from all kinds of different backgrounds, sharing wine together as well as food. What do you think his favourite foods were?

Something to share

Pack and imaginary picnic basket. Take it in turns to choose and add items to the basket for everyone.

36

EASTER GARDEN

Make an 'Easter Garden' by creating a photo collage. Take some pictures of various different flowers, perhaps from your own garden or as you walk around your local area. Then use an online tool to arrange them into a beautiful Easter garden collage. You might like to add some words such as 'He Is Risen!', 'Jesus is Alive!' or 'Blessings at Easter' and send the picture as a message to friends and family.

Something to pray

Lord Jesus,
as we look at the flowers around us
so many colours,
shapes
and sizes,
with leaves of different greens,
we remember the garden

where you appeared
to your friends
and are thankful
that so often
we meet you in a garden too.

Amen.

Something to wonder about

Why do flowers look beautiful to us? Do you prefer wild flowers or cultivated flowers, and why?

Something to share

Collect some small flowers, if you can, between you, and put them in some water in a jam jar. You might like to share a photo of this with friends or family.

37

LIGHT

Reuse a piece of clear plastic by covering it with glue, and sticking colourful cut-out tissue paper flowers all over it until it is completely covered. Then, cut a cross shaped hole out from the middle of two pieces of black card (make sure that both are in the same position), and sandwich the colourful flowery plastic in between. If you put this in your window, the light will shine through. In the daytime it can be seen from the inside, and at night it will be lit up for those to see who are passing by.

Something to pray

Jesus,
may your light shine
in our lives
for all to see
so that we may show
your love

and grace
in our community.

Amen.

Something to wonder about

What are the factors which help the light to shine through the flowery window-picture, and what stops it? Are there any similarities with things in our lives?

Something to share

Who or what would you like to see a picture of in a stained glass window?

38

THE CROSS

Using two sticks and some different coloured scraps of wool (or rainbow wool), create a 'Mexican God's Eye':

1. Tie the two sticks together to make a cross shape, and attach the wool to the middle.
2. Wrap your yarn around one stick, close to the center of the God's eye, then take it over to the next stick, wrap it around this one, and so on, doing the same with each stick.
3. Continue to wrap the yarn around the sticks like this, rotating the cross as you work.

You should find that a smooth pattern starts to form on one side of the cross, as the strands of wool lie next to each other.

Use this activity as a chance to reflect on the themes of Easter – finding hope in the middle of despair, love that triumphs over hate, and life over death.

Something to pray

With the cross
at the centre
we focus on you.

May our lives
weave a pattern
of the kind things
we do.

Amen.

Something to wonder about

How does it make you feel to think about, look at or hold the cross? Why do you think this is?

Something to share

The themes of Easter are found in both religious and non-religious settings. What other stories, films or songs reveal our need as humans to hear about good triumphing over evil, light over darkness, and life over death?

39

RESURRECTION

Hard boil some eggs, leave them to cool and dry, and use coloured pens to decorate them. Add brightly coloured swirls, lines or wedges of colour to the egg, until it is completely covered. On top of this, use a plain colour to draw a cross shape on top, and add the words 'He is Risen!' You could put these in lunchboxes, give them to friends or take them on a picnic.

Something to pray

Round like a stone,
smooth and lifeless . . .

Who would believe
that out of an egg
could hatch
a tiny baby bird?

Thank you, dear Lord,
that when things seem hopeless
or impossible
we can come to you in prayer.

And that you will show us the way,
bringing hope and healing,
wisdom, courage and strength,
with joy and blessing
as we go.

Amen.

Something to wonder about

Imagine you were inside a big eggshell, and you hadn't seen the world outside. What would it be like, as you broke your way out?

Something to share

If you could hatch some eggs out, what would you choose? Dragons, flamingos, eagles, penguins, dinosaurs, or something else?

40

FLOWERS

Fill your house with flowers – jars of dandelions, jugs of daffodils, reduced-price bunches of flowers from the supermarket, or paper flowers made from recycled materials.

Put these together in one place, with a few candles safely placed around them, to create a focus for prayer and reflection on the night of Maundy Thursday (or another day if this works better for you). Then on Easter Day, enjoy the flowers as a table centrepiece as you eat your meals.

Something to pray

Dear God,
the pinks, yellows, creams and blues,
and the delicate shapes
of springtime flowers,
bring colour,
refreshment
and joy,

reminding us
of your creativity,
your generosity
and your love.

Amen.

Something to wonder about

How can flowers and plants help us to reflect, and focus on God?

Something to share

If you could create a garden however you wanted, what would you put in it? Waterfalls, different colour flowers, places to climb? Or perhaps a home for nature, a pond, or somewhere to play?

About the Author

ELEANOR KING

Eleanor lives by the seaside in Essex with her husband and three children, and buckets and spades on the doorstep. She spends a lot of time running different groups in the community, both inside and outside the church, but when she is not doing this she likes to make biscuits, go walking and knit or crochet things that are not too big or complicated.

Looking for more resources?

ALSO BY ELEANOR KING

ISBN: 978-1-8486-7945-0

Marble-run prayers, milkshake prayers, paper boat prayers and teapot prayers – there's something for everyone in this fun, thought-provoking and creative book. vThe prayer ideas are grouped into five themes:

- Saying thank you
- Sorry prayers
- Prayers for others
- Prayers for ourselves
- Things to remind us to pray